DRAFT OF A LETTER

PHOENIX POETS

Draft of a Letter

JAMES LONGENBACH

THE UNIVERSITY OF CHICAGO PRESS
Chicago and London

JAMES LONGENBACH is the Joseph Henry Gilmore
Professor of English at the University of Rochester. He is the
author of two books of poems, *Threshold* and *Fleet River*, as well
as five critical studies of modern literature, most recently *The
Resistance to Poetry*.

The University of Chicago Press, Chicago 60637
The University of Chicago Press, Ltd., London
© 2007 by The University of Chicago
All rights reserved. Published 2007
Printed in the United States of America

16 15 14 13 12 11 10 09 08 07   1 2 3 4 5

ISBN-13: 978-0-226-49268-1 (paper)
ISBN-10: 0-226-49268-0 (paper)

Library of Congress Cataloging-in-Publication Data

Longenbach, James.
  Draft of a letter / James Longenbach.
     p. cm. — (Phoenix poets)
  ISBN-13: 978-0-226-49268-1 (pbk. : alk. paper)
  ISBN-10: 0-226-49268-0 (pbk. : alk. paper)
  I. Title. II. Series.
  PS3562.O4967D73 2007
  813'.54—dc22
                                        2006010060

to Joanna

Drowned is reason that should me consort,
And I remain dispering of the port.

— WYATT, AFTER PETRARCH

Contents

Acknowledgments

Grateful acknowledgment is made to the editors of publications in which these poems first appeared.

American Poet: "Reason and Sorrow"
The American Scholar: "Sparrow," "Seond Draft," Volume 75, No. 2, Spring 2006
Boston Review: "Death and Reason," "The Gift"
The Nation: "Buried Life"
New England Review: "Self and Soul" ("When you reach the cliffs")
The Paris Review: "Complaint"
Raritan: "Swallowtail"
Salmagundi: "Self and Soul" ("Do you see that field"), "Testament"
Slate: "Draft of a Letter," "The Gods in Exile"
Southwest Review: "Abacus," Volume 90, Number 4, 2005
Subtropics: "Ghost Pond"
TriQuarterly: "Canzone," "Ice Men," "Joy and Reason," "Tenzone"
The Yale Review: "Yard Work," "A Different Route," Vol. 93 no. 3 and Vol. 94 no. 4

I

Ice Men

One cuts blocks
From the abundant river,
Hauls them house to house.

One falls, unseen,
The heart
Inoculated cold

Against a sky still moving.
Moving even now
Above the river,
The canal.
Willows shimmering

Across the water,
Muskrats diving out of reach.
The river whispers
Till it freezes—

A body
Twirling sluggishly
Beneath the surface as again

One stacks, then
Spreads the straw.

Another falters,
Slips, or
Puts a sliver on your tongue
To feel it melting there—
The ice-lit

Underworld
Of someone else.

Death and Reason

Path shifting in the woods
With sunlight, darkness, and at dusk
The little voices
Returning to their nests.

First rule: there is
Someone else.

Towee, towee
Repeated in the trees
Behind the shopping mall,
Tiny breaths escaping from the larynx—
Follow me, follow me—
A knothole: two eyes
Glistening,
Smaller than yours.
They vanish when a cloud slips past.

Second rule: the presence
Of other people
Proves you're alive.

Beyond the arbor,
Scent of the lilacs, footprints
Leading from the kitchen
Over the dry grass, silver, moonlit—

Before the light turns
Indigo, nothing between
Your face and finitude, the long
Time you will live a place
You don't live now—

First rule.

They sing, their black
Eyes flickering.

Draft of a Letter

As a young man
I was blessed with a body
Not of great strength
But very agile.

My torso,
Thin from the start,
Grew wiry as I ran.
The pleasure

I derived from straightening
My room I never
Learned to will.
I feel it now.

In time,
Without trying,
I found a rhythm
Of thought ineffably
Hesitant, serene. Clouds

From the invisible
Mountain top,
Then mist.
Rain soaked the ground
Until it swelled,

Lifting
My body

Flat on its back.
Delicate fingers,
Voice fair.
In the end

I found myself drawn
To what was neither very large

Nor very small.
If you say the word death
In heaven,
Nobody understands.

The Gift

Sparrows at the feeder.
Rain in the leaves.

From deepest darkness to
The lesser I emerged with the words

I don't believe

Immediately in my mouth.
I didn't speak.

*

Yellow leaves,
Red berries.
Berries

Of my childhood strung
On a slender branch.
From what immensity did they

Emerge, what context,
What scene?

I tried
To read me.
Propped myself

Against the pillow.
Moved my lips.

*

If you bring it forth,
What is within you

Will save you.
What is not within you—

*

Hair on the pillow.
Voices in the leaves.

I asked *in what*—

They said *in you in you in you in you*—

I was capable
Of speaking truth. I had

The truth but
Nothing to put it in.

Rain in the leaves.
A company
Passing invisible.

Don't ask why.

*

For twenty years I lived in the present.
Then, in a single night,
I became a shade.

Books, paintings
On the wall,
Words in my mouth but no

Memory, no need.
I listened

To the sparrows.
Happiness without reason.
Yellow leaves.

Canzone

Each day, when sunlight
Flees to other people,
A woman rests
Her load of bracken on the road.
When shadows descend

From the tallest mountain,
Darkening the fields,
A farmer collects his tools.
A shepherd reaches for his staff.
He lays green branches
In a cave while out at sea

The mariner reclines
On hard wood,
Ropes loosening,
The sails calm.
Oxen return
Unharnessed
From the fields—

Why is my yoke never lifted?
If being mine from morning to night
Has earned me sympathy, poem,
Don't show yourself.
Move from hill to hill

Remembering
How the living stone
On which I lean
Outlasts me,
Reduces me to ash.

Joy and Reason

I am sailing happily.

Bait for shipwreck.
People who dash about on
Battlements, yardarms of ships,
Are betrayed by level roads.
The first age has spurs,
The last a bridle.

The surface is calm.
My swiftness is unheard of.

Your throat will wrinkle.
Lines will furrow your soft cheeks
And the brightness of your eyes
Will be covered by a cloud.
With the man who said virtue
Is more pleasing in fine
Forms, I can't agree.

Right now, at least, my body is exceptional.
It is admired by everyone.

Whence this avalanche of water,
These billowing waves?
When what remains

Of your hair has fallen out,
Your shoulders bent,
Hands withered
And the radiant ivory
Of your teeth turned black,
You will recognize yourself.

I have sailed prosperously.
I am already on shore.

Buried Life

Imagine cities you've
Inhabited, streets
Paved in lava stone.
You never intended to pray

In the temples, had
Nothing to sell.
Now imagine yourself

Returning to those same cities.
Hunt for people you knew,
Knock on their doors.
Ask yourself

Where are the vases, animals
Etched in gold?
Where are the wines

From distant places,
Banquets ferreted
From the bowels of the earth?
While you were missing

Other people wore
Your garments,
Slept in your bed.

How frightening
The man who said
In his affliction

Wood has hope.
Cut down
It will flourish.

If the root grows old
And the trunk withers
In dust, at the scent of water
It will germinate.

O Tourist

for Kenneth Gross

I.

Once having built
His house, little door
No higher than his head,
He found himself

Floating in the bay.
Boats rocked back and forth
In the marina and the water grew

A deeper, lustier green.
He remembers

His sneakers,
The way they poked
From the bottom of his jeans
As if he were sleeping,
Ready to get up.

2.

He left himself behind.
Two children rolled a ball
Along the quay—they moved

Their fingers expertly
And he stood still.
Mind ordering itself as it wills
The body; mind refusing what it wills.
A wall, and through the keyhole

Rows of cypress
Though there weren't two
Sides, there were millions: flock

Of blackbirds rising from the branches,
Children chasing one another,
Clambering
Against the wall

But he couldn't see them.
They were on the other side.

Whether it was the voice of a boy
Or a girl he couldn't say.
It shouted *open it*.

3.

Couples eating breakfast,
Speaking softly
Though with nothing to hide.
My mother died last year.

Juniper, rosemary so fragrant
He snipped a piece
And laid it on his plate.

*After driving through the mountains
It was hard to breathe.*

Around the tables
Lemon trees in pots, the garden
Parched around the edges, irrigated.
Tiny insects hovering

Above the sugar bowls,
The different juices.
I was never alone.

4.

He put down roots.
He bought a dictionary—then,
Because it was on sale, underwear.

Wounded. Arrive.
He wandered

Freely among women in velvet dresses,
Men in cutaways: the movement
Of their bodies
Vivid, spindly thighs.

One bowed. One lifted
Fingers to his lips.

Until he left for his own country
By a different route
He'd never worn
These boxers, slightly

Elastic, little legs.
I am wounded,
I want to leave this place—

5.

When Jonah fled to Tarshish
From the presence of the Lord

The Lord sent out a tempest.
The mariners were afraid.
Arise, go.
They threw the contents of the ship into the sea

While Jonah slept.

6.

When he came back
He found a cup of instant on the counter.
Laundry glistening with rain.

The sunken harbor,
Boats lined
Belly-up along the quay—

A black Mercedes
Squeezed him to the railing
But he didn't flinch; he chewed
An apple to the core, then

Dropped it,
Watched it fall.

The silver branches,
Burning vines.
White core floating in the bay

Half eaten,
Half expelled.

Self and Soul

Do you see that field
Beyond the tennis court,
Poppies floating in a golden cloud?
Unbutton your shirt.
Bask in the sun.

Grass withers,
Flowers fade.

A fountain trickles
To a shell, then fills a pool.
Goats are sporting
In the clover while in heaven
Objects never cease
To be themselves.

In heaven you
Wouldn't exist.

Imagine water rising
From the ground,
Then falling back again, each drop
A pendant, then a stain.
If the kingdom is in the sky
Birds will get there before you.

Split open a piece of wood.
Lift up a stone.

You grimace
When you serve.

What drew the shepherd of Etna
From his cave but
Sunlight on a day like this,
Poppies in front of him,
Bones behind?

The Gods in Exile

One grew into a pear tree,
Bearing fruit.
Another, dissatisfied

With created things,
Withdrew: chameleon
Blending with the branch. Climbing

Their stairs, I saw complete
What they'd seen
Rising: a dome,
An intelligence
Hovering above the streets

To cover us all.
Highways, strip malls.
Hercules lifting Antaeus

Pelvis to pelvis,
Earth to earth.

One became a sparrow,
Joined the flock.
When his singing aroused
Suspicion, he exchanged his voice

For a peacock's,
The solitary
Darkness of God.

One became a river.
One raised sheep.

Ghost Pond

A sack with a hole.
A tree without roots.

Desert of sand.
Dust that blinds.

Lake beside the graveyard.
White swan frozen in the lake—

I skated past it,
Circled back.

*

No color, all brushwork.
Room full of smoke.

There was a hand before my face and
I took it, I lived after dark.
When it withdrew

I lay down in the snow.
The will to touch,

To feel, answering
The deepest human wish.

Not blankness;
Richness of texture.

*

Two rules about thin ice.
You can skate so long as you move

Quickly, never stop.
If you fall in

Look up.
Circle of light.

*

It passes like the moon.
It turns like a wheel.

Field of stones.
City of blood.

An ocean without a harbor.
Bait without a hook.

*

One hand pressed
Against my spine,

One to my chest, she tilted me
Back until the water lapped my head.

Willows dangling,
Oaks retreating—

Why do souls rise from here?
How could they crave daylight?

I reached up to embrace her
Three times.
Nothing but air.

The root of need
Is plenitude, she said.

Then she embraced
My head and pulled me under.

Swallowtail

Leaves, a pattern
Of stars between overlapping
Locust and pine—

I woke up on a gurney
Covered with wires.
I was breathing

But my chest was burned: seconds
Creeping past me in a row.
Organs, arteries, thousands of intersecting parts.

Your hair was cut shorter then.
In time, I liked my second
Body better
Than the first.

2.

When an insect assumes
A different shape,
A form,

It doesn't deceive;
It becomes a different
Version of itself.
Swallowtail

Lilting through a field
Of Queen Anne's lace, light
Reflecting up from earth, returning

Through the veined
Transparence
Of wings—

When I opened my eyes at first
I saw nothing.
I heard footsteps
                    ta tum ta tum
My heartbeat running back to me—your

Arms around me,
Tangle of wires.
I watched you

Watch me
Taking shape.

3.

At first there were many of them.
They slept in hammocks
Dangling from the trees.
Their bodies grew

But couldn't change,
Then changed
But couldn't exist—they were

Already missing:
Canvas hanging stiff,
A split cocoon.

In time, a few returned.
Light between the branches
Flickering, but sure.

Who am I, moving towards you?
Who are you?

II

Reason and Sorrow

Now that you're here,
Happy with the sprig of mint
In your aperitif,
I'm happy too. Remember
How I rubbed your feet with oil?

My house is too big.

Although I led you across
Verdant meadows,
Undulant seas,
It couldn't have been more difficult.
I wanted to get us lost.

My stomach is full.
I never left home.

Walking together
Side by side,
The mind more stilled than ever
In its little nest—

How can I be happy if
The one who suffers isn't me?

Already the grapes are harvested,
The lavender bundled in rows.
I've made a savarin,
White sugar
Dusted with gold.

Complaint

The newborn bear has no shape.
The mule rarely gives birth,
The viper only once.
Alone among all things

The crocodile moves its upper jaw.
Moles are deaf, bees blind,
The elephant dies standing,
The phoenix is consumed by fire.

If a bat goes hungry it feeds
From the mouths of other bats.
If tigers are stunned with a mirror
They drop their prey.

Whales may lie on their backs for days,
Deceiving ships.
With twenty arms the cuttlefish
Clasps a drowning man

Like highwaymen for whom
The final gasp of air
Becomes the one
Possession worth stealing

From the peddler who has
Nothing but thoughts.
What came to his mind
Sprang first from his mouth.

Friends, whoever reads this,
Know that I am sitting on a bench
Beside the lower paddock,
Rowing against the current.

Second Draft

As an older man,
Graying, not stooped,
I saw the future:
Extremities

Cold, tongue
Sluggish,
Foam at the lips.
Excessive hope

Seemed more
Indulgent
Than despair.
I ran great distances.
I stood in sunlight

Just to see my shadow,
Show it off.
For the first time I remember

My soul looked back.
What other people learn
From birth,
Betrayal,
I learned late.

My soul perched
On an olive branch
Combing itself,
Waving its plumes. I said

Being mortal,
I aspire to
Mortal things.

I need you,
Said my soul,
If you're telling the truth.

Abacus

Forty-nine, forty-eight—
Our daughters won't be

Children forever.
What do I see?

Black dog bounding through the grass, then gone.
The yellow house.
Palm trees bent with snow. The sea

Below Mohegan Bluffs—
Cold sand on my knees beside
You as the sun rose
Blind, aloof—

One was born frowning.
The other screamed.

2.

Look down
Through winter branches to the roof,
The attic room where I reclaimed
This lamp, this desk

My father made,
Muttering
Beneath my breath

Pentameters—*she has*
Green eyes but
Wears a hood that hides them—

Six apartments,
Five cities,
Two continents: the red

We rented and the blue we
Borrowed but
The yellow house

We built.

Taller than a sycamore,
Taller than the place I came from.
Look up.

3.

My second lifetime,
When did it begin?
Each year a bell.

I stood beside a yucca plant:
White spike
Of blossoms bending
From its weight,
Cells dying
By the million,
Sloughed, replaced—by listening

I was changed forever,
Forever the same.
The flower didn't speak to me but
I spoke back, I heard

My name.
I was
Our second daughter's age.

Locust shells.
Petals.
Number of times I've

Told this story,
Trochee, dactyl—
Stresses in her name.

4.

Spirit of the river,
Spirit of the sea.

Because we want to be children forever
I ran the stoplights whispering
To myself
Alone in the dark car.

Nineteen, eighteen—
Skills we practice for a lifetime
Disappearing
In a single turn: fingers

On the keyboard self-delighting.
House in which I write this.
Pebbles in the sea.

At thirteen she is
Taller than her mother.

Spirit of the sand beneath us.
Spirit of the tree.

Tenzone

Look at your reflection.
How do I greet
Someone you've never seen?

Today, the apples are ripe,
The chestnuts splitting their hulls.

A spring that's fouled.
A mirror that's stained.

Are you saying I can't drink the water?

I'm saying you'll find out
When you're dying.
Desert of sand.
A ship that leaks.

You're the one trespassing.

A cloud against the sun.
Old age without a stick.

You'll be mine or
I will be yours.
No kicking or gouging.

Those are the rules
Of cock fights.
If you still don't believe me—

Give me your finger.
Touch my scar.

Yard Work

Without question
There are means; and equally
Beyond equivocation

There is no end.
I tied a noose

Around a hemlock grown too large and
Sawed until it staggered
To the ground.

Hear me

Said the branches leaning down
To cover what stilled them.
I dipped a cup

Into the spring,
Water striders scurrying
Beneath the mosses

And I had no thirst.
I stripped the branches,
Sawed the trunk in pieces small
Enough to burn—

Hear me
Look at me

This is the time of year we find
Our bodies lost
In bodies
Larger than we'd thought.

First rule: no one
Is speaking. The second is
Follow the sound.

Sparrow

I wanted never to sing again
For I was not understood,
I was scorned.
Anyone can be miserable in a public place.

He who has lost his way,
Let him turn back.
He who has no dwelling,
Let him sleep on the grass.

I hear that Phaeton fell in the Po and died.
The proverb "love him who loves you"
Is an ancient thing.
I know what I'm saying.

One travels a long way to be safe.
He who sets the net
Doesn't always catch fish,
He who is subtle may break his neck.

Blessed be the key that turned in my heart,
Released my soul and
Freed it from a heavy chain.
Violets at night along the shore.

Across the Apennines,
Languorous surf,
Palm trees lining the beaches, cliffs, a portal
Narrowing to a tiny room, no ore,

Just limestone,
Water-smooth—
A sparrow hastened
To my dwelling place:

The sound of the sea is other people.
Where once you sorrowed
Somebody else now sorrows,
Making sorrow sweet.

Some answer when no one calls.
Some flee from those who beg.
In whose name do you sing, I asked,
What love brought you here?

Second Life

Accompanied
To the Campi Flegrei
By a shadow,

She listened to voices rise
From the darkness,
Then recede.

Instruments
Sustained them.
When one had finished

Others played.
False proportions
Sung boldly.

Rain on the roof tiles.
O selve, o campi.

A Different Route

for Marguerite and Peter Casparian

1.

Life in our country proved
Too much for me.
The roar of outrage,
Menace of fortune—
Waves and cliffs on every side.

Finally, what I'd hoped for
Came to pass.
A little wine, then

Silence, secret friends
From every century—
They take up
Only a small corner of the house.

Some teach me to endure,
Others to have no
Longing.
An indescribable

Sweetness,
Like heaven.

2.

You were with me.
Also the children
Who were little again.
Monsieur Chien each morning

Begging for scraps.
Rain scoured the hills.
A pool beside the cottage
Overflowed in tiny
Rivulets—

Water striders,
Filaments of blue slime.
Someone had built this place by hand.

Across the ocean thousands
Of miles away,
America was gathering its hosts.
Small countries
Were persuaded to join.

But you were with me.
Also your mother,
Who was driven from the cemetery
By a man in a wool cap,
Speaking French.

3.

We followed the stream
Higher, into the hills,
All five of us. The path grew

Narrow, slippery,
Until we passed a gate.
Lavender bloomed in the crevices.
Porte de Paradis
Read the sign.

That part is true.
What happened next

I can explain only
By risking foolishness.
Though we were climbing higher

The stream grew wide,
Spreading out as on a plain.
The water crystalline, cold, flowing
Swiftly so the long green reeds
Reached out as if pleading,
Begging for more.
At the source

The bulk of water
Lifted itself from the earth
Like molten glass—
Slowly, but with great force.
I saw anchorite caves

In the cliff side.
I'd lived there before.

4.

Deep in the wood
A fountain welled from stone,
Fresh water murmuring.

To that hidden place,
Shaded and cool,
No shepherds came, no goatherds.
Only nymphs and muses
Joining together in song.

I seated myself.
And when I had tasted the sweetness
Of their singing,
Of the place,

I saw a chasm open
In the earth.
It swallowed the fountain,
Leaving me to grieve. Even today

This memory
Fills me with fear.

5.

Streets uncurling
From the church,
The ironwork steeple,
Ivy covering the town hall clock—
We circled the village
One last time.

Laughter from a café table.
Candlelight flickering in a globe.
I didn't recognize their faces

But they beckoned,
Poured us wine.
And for an hour

We didn't look forward,
We didn't look back.
No need to care

About our children
Sleeping in their beds,
Your mother standing
By the cottage in her nightgown,
Calling our names.

Self and Soul

When you reach the cliffs
Defended by Manlius
Enter the sea.

Who finds
Tranquility
Where he was born?

*

The star he wished on.
The sea where he fished.

Night he invaded.
The guards who slept.

*

Follow the river past
Stony plains
Until you reach
The fount: gorse, clear water

Spilling from beneath granite shelves.
No pinnacle
But the view immense.

A breeze from nowhere
Ruffling the leaves.

*

The sparrows he fashioned.
The friends he lost.

*

This is the place where
Jesus was hidden from Herod's fury.
Believers drink greedily

But for the rest of us
A drop on the tongue is
Hard punishment.

*

Who stilled the wind.
Who sighted the blind.

Stupefied shepherds.
Conqueror of death.

*

You'll carry not
My portrait, like a lover,
But this account of what you'll see
By someone who's never

Seen it, never will.
I'll be standing on the right

As you're leaving,
The left
If you return.

Testament

Before death should prevent me,
I dispose of my self,
My soul, and my possessions.
Don't return me

To earth, a burden.
Make me smoke.
Recite an alphabet

Of lamentations.
Aleph, beth, gimel—
Jerusalem, return to the Lord your God.

Float me on the dark canal.
Then watch the lights
Of the Giudecca glittering
Across the water.
If I'm lucky

It will be winter,
When the lights are prettiest.
Maybe a little snow.

Don't remember me angry
Or short-tempered;
It was difficult

For me to speak.
Remember my parents.
When I first saw heaven

One of you frowned,
One screamed.
In the Temple of Fortune

Built by Telegonus,
Son of Circe,
Last child of Odysseus,
One of you was sitting in an olive tree.

After Petrarch

How often, in summer,
Did I rise at midnight?
How often did the darkness find me

Now upon the mountain,
Now by the sea?

I measured the deserted fields
With my steps, my eyes
Alert for anyone's footprint
Marking the sand.
No other shield

Protects me from people's knowledge.
My body
Anyone can read.

How often, at that hour,
Did I enter the cave
From which the river emerges,
A place I dread entering

Even by day?
I believe that by now

Mountains and rivers
Know the temper of my life.
I can't find paths

Harsh enough,
Savage enough,
That my soul does not
Lift me with talking while
Listening to mine.

Note

The fourth section of "A Different Route" is a loose translation of the fourth
stanza of poem 323 from Petrarch's *Canzoniere*. "Canzone," "Sparrow," and
"After Petrarch" contain several lines translated from poems 35, 50, and 105.
More generally, the poems are indebted to the Latin prose works of Petrarch.
More specifically, the third section of "The Gift" is adapted from the "Gospel of
Thomas" in the *Nag Hammadi Library*, as are lines in the fifth stanza of the first
"Self and Soul." The final line of "Second Life" ("o woods, o fields") is taken
from Ottavio Rinuccini's libretto for Jacopo Peri's *Euridice*.